Tales of a Borderline

Rebecca Aspey

Presentation by *BookLeaf Publishing*

Web: www.bookleafpub.com

E-mail: info@bookleafpub.com

ISBN: 9789357696883

First edition 2022

DEDICATION

This book is dedicated to my younger self, my self who never stopped believing that one day, we could create something like this.

Polluted Love

How gloomy is it, my dear,
that the world we once knew of will slowly
disappear?
That the cerulean sky will fade to an ash grey
and the flora around us will start to slowly
decay?

How gloomy is it, my dear,
that the once unsoiled ocean will no longer
remain clean?
That the pollution of our minds will fill the
waves
and the butterflies and bees will fall violently
into their graves?

How gloomy is it, my dear,
that the love we held so close will turn
insincere?
That the volume of our voices will raise above
the atmosphere
and will break our hearts and leave the pieces
scattered here?

Lifeless

I don't have any stories to tell,
there are no laughter lines beside my eyes,
there are no scars upon my skin.
I have nothing to showcase,
I have nothing to spare.
No calluses sit on my fingertips,
no scrapes litter my knees.
There are no childhood drawings,
there are no memories made.
I don't have any stories to share,
I live under stones,
they crush me with every breath.
Never free to leave my cave,
never free to walk this earth.
I have never felt the grass beneath my feet,
I have never felt the seaside breeze.
There are no tears in the soles of my shoes,
it was like I was never here,
it was like I was never there.

Metanoia

I travelled for so long,
my legs turned to dust.
I could hear the skies sing me a lullaby,
I could feel the earth hum back under my feet.

Turning my head, I decided,
now was my time to leave.
I could hear the snake hissing my name,
but I just turned my head and walked away.

For he didn't have control over me anymore.
He could hiss and bite with everything he has,
but I would never turn my head and come back.

So, I continued on my journey,
and my legs turned to dust.
Just this one moment to myself,
just this one adventure all on my own.

The Insider

You glance longingly out of tightly shut windows,
how long have you been hidden away from the
world?
It must have been days, weeks, or even months
since you last presented yourself to society.

Your heart begins to race as you ponder the world
visible behind your windowsill,
it's not fair, you've been stuck here for so long.
The world is a beautiful place, yet you fear stepping
into it,
yet you fear embracing it for all its glory and light.

How much longer do you need to spend inside?
You've been hidden for so long, yet you never break,
yet you never open your wings and fly away.

Will you eventually exit this dreadful place,
or will you forever remain as the insider?

Sympathy From The Devil

The Devil sat me on their lap
and spoke to me a story of darkness.
They held out an open hand for me to hold
and brushed my hair away gently.

It was a story I had heard before,
one I had lived and learned from.
The Devil spoke of evil men and broken trust,
they spoke of everything I had lost.

I felt the Devil's sympathy in their words,
I felt the sadness and the rage.
Just how much did he have to mess up
for the Devil to side with me?

Daydreamer

Sometimes I like to pretend I live in a whole other world,
a world where you do not exist,
a world where no one I know exists.
It makes it easier to deal with the everlasting pain,
a pain which fills my insides with burning fire,
a pain that holds me hostage inside my room.

Sometimes I like to daydream about speaking with you,
speaking about what happened,
speaking that always seems to end with my anger.
It makes it harder to deal with the everlasting pain,
it reminds me of how enraged I have been,
it reminds me of all the bottled-up emotions inside me.

Sometimes I like to pretend you don't exist,
like we've never spoken before,
like we would never even meet.
It tends to ease the pain for a little while,
it loosens the rope constricting my chest,
it frees my brain from the dark clouds polluting it.

Sometimes I like to imagine life if you never hurt me,
life filled with love and laughter,
life where we could be a family.
It brings the pain back to the front of my mind,
it chokes me and shakes me to my core,
it fills me with dread and anger.

And so,
it is easier to pretend I live in a whole other world,
a world where both you and I do not exist.

Poisonous Love

The angel would walk through hell
if it meant she could be with the demon.

She would lower the clouds and sing to the heavens
if it meant she could speak to the demon.

She would slice off her own wings, permanently
stuck on the ground
if it meant she could love the demon,
one
last
time.

Humans

Humans.
If you glance at them the right way, you will notice the desire within them to become something different; something better. Fighting with themselves over the flaws they are covered in - they must become impeccable, untarnished, exemplary; perfect.

Humans.
The sinful, unclean bastards striving for something better, something useful - considering their worth, their values, and their destiny to be worthless if they are without perfection.

But what is perfection?
Is it nothing more than a feeling?
When will perfect truly be enough for their ideals?
Is perfection nothing more than flawlessness?

Humans.
Aiming for the unrealistic outcome of perfection - no matter what they choose to do or who they believe they are destined to become, perfection will never be enough.

Humans.
They will keep fighting for the unattainable, murdering themselves to achieve this ideal lifestyle that not a single other human owns.

I truly hate perfection.

Fight For You

When your inspiration is not visible.
When you take the stairs just to miss them all.
When your eyes won't obey your head.
When it seems as though all your confidence has fled.

When your chest is badly aching.
When your body will just not stop shaking.
When your lungs won't help you breathe.
When it feels like all people ever do is leave.

When the sky just never seems to brighten.
When your eyes won't stop crying.
When your heart refuses to obey your head.
When your body is filled to the brim with dread.

When you feel like you're not loved.
When the others do nothing but judge.
When your brain is filled with rage and anger.
When the person you see in the mirror is a stranger.

I will fight for you.

Quarantine Routine

How does one cope with no routine?
it never made much sense to me.
My mind gets all torn up,
my brain aches for structure in order to feel free.

How does one cope with no tasks?
it never made much sense in my mind.
The days seem pointless and weak,
a day without tasks has me feeling blind.

How does one cope with no medication?
it has never made much sense to me.
Without it I am dazed and confused,
I'm trapped in my thoughts, unable to be free.

How does one cope with no routine?
I swear it will never make sense to me.
My brain is divergent,
so my thoughts will continue to scream.

Always Missing You

Is it wrong to say, "I miss you"?
Is is bad to say, "I care"?
Should I leave and face the truth
or should I pretend you were never there?

Is it wrong to invite you over?
Is it bad to wish you'd come?
Should I leave you feeling colder
or should I pretend I don't wish to feel numb?

Because my mind doesn't understand,
what my heart, it aches to have.
My lungs, they always burn up,
as you say, "you're not enough."

Withered

These flowers
don't bloom around here anymore.
They once grew beautifully,
rising from the ground.
But lately,
all the flowers have withered away and died.
And maybe,
just maybe,
it was my own fault.

Falling Behind

It was the feeling you would get after seeing someone you knew from high school working an important and fulfilling full-time job. It was the feeling you would get after comparing all those old acquaintances to your own life outside of school. It was the feeling of being frozen into place, never truly being able to catch up with the others; constantly behind. Never finishing University; never finishing anything you start.

It was the feeling that you were always destined to become a late bloomer, a failure, behind in life, or anything else your brain could trick you into believing about yourself.

It was a feeling that would creep up out of the dark sometimes. The feeling would always show itself just as you were beginning to feel satisfied, proud, and free. It was the type of feeling that caused you to panic and spiral; never a helpful feeling.

Motivation seemed meaningless, and all the wasted time and effort spent studying for courses that you would end up quitting in the long run, seemed to destroy you slowly over time. Racking up debt, for which in the end, would mean nothing.

Oh, how painful it is to be a gifted child turned into a burnout of an adult. From a child with potential, to an adult with wasted knowledge.

Numb

I tried to describe how I felt,
but the paper remained blank
as did my eyes and my heart.

I tried to show you how I live,
but all we did was lay in bed
until the sky turned dark.

Unlovable

15

I just don't think love is for me,
every time I fall it ends in anger.
Things seem to go well for a little while,
until the feelings fade and it becomes harder to show
you a smile.

I just don't think love is for me,
the constant anxiety is deafening.
Always worried I've done something wrong.
Message me differently and all of a sudden I don't
believe we truly belong.

Perhaps I'm just unlovable.

Oneirataxia

Sometimes when I close my eyes
I drift silently toward a whole other world.
The memories I make in this world
collide with my memories of reality.
It can warp my sense of direction,
it pulls me from side to side.
These false memories that fill my mind
cause me to ache and make me cry.

Sometimes when my eyes are open
I still can't stop myself from drifting.
I create new memories inside my mind
that just aren't real, they're all lies.
These false realities can be comforting though,
they can help me escape from my truths.
There is however, one pressing issue,
I no longer recognise what is real and true.

Clinomania

17

Cover me in warmness, clench my frozen heart.
If not for these safety blankets, I believe I would fall apart.
Smother me in the sheets, calm my racing mind.
If it weren't for the silence of my solitude,
my thoughts would eat me alive.

Unwanted Acquaintance

18

Tragedy is one thing she is no stranger to.
Her lungs inhale pain and suffering,
they exhale happiness and laughter.

Tragedy is funny like that,
he can warp your oxygen into cyanide,
grind your bones into dust.

Tragedy is one thing she is no stranger to,
but she does wish she never met him.

Close Friends

Emptiness is a friend of mine,
I met him once and he decided to stay forever.
He braids my hair with twine,
he holds my hand during my endeavours.

Emptiness was there for me through it all,
he cheered me on when things got difficult.
He would never yell or scream at me,
he would keep his opinions equivocal.

Emptiness is a friend of mine,
I met him once and he decided he would never leave.

Black and White

I'll paint my face to match yours,
I'll change my clothes and my hair.
I'll switch the way I speak and walk,
I'll change anything to ensure that you care.

I'll laugh at the bad jokes you spill,
I'll match my identity to fit your liking.
I'll switch my hobbies for yours,
I'll do anything to prevent us from fighting.

And when we fight,
I'll just get up and walk away.
I'll pretend I never knew you,
because in my mind, I was betrayed.

Growth

The flower will continue to grow and thrive, no
matter what life throws her way.
She won't let her past control her future, and in the
end, she will be okay.